LEONARD
ANE
CITY OF I

by Myka-Lynne Sokoloff

Harcourt
SCHOOL PUBLISHERS

ISBN 10: 0-15-350546-X
ISBN 13: 978-0-15-350546-1

Ordering Options
ISBN 10: 0-15-350335-1 (Grade 5 Below-Level Collection)
ISBN 13: 978-0-15-350335-1 (Grade 5 Below-Level Collection)
ISBN 10: 0-15-357544-1 (package of 5)
ISBN 13: 978-0-15-357544-0 (package of 5)

11 12 13 14 15   0940   12 11 10

Leonardo da Vinci is often called a Renaissance Man. This means that he had many different skills and interests. They ranged from art to science to the world of ideas.

The word *Renaissance* means "rebirth." It names a time in history. The Renaissance took place from the 1200s to the 1600s. This period saw a rebirth in art, science, thinking, and exploration. People rediscovered many ideas from ancient Greece and Rome. They also created many new things.

In Leonardo's time, Florence, Italy, was the most important city in Europe. In fact, the city is called the birthplace of the Renaissance. Leonardo lived there for many years.

What would life have been like if you lived in a Renaissance city? Let's take a look and find out.

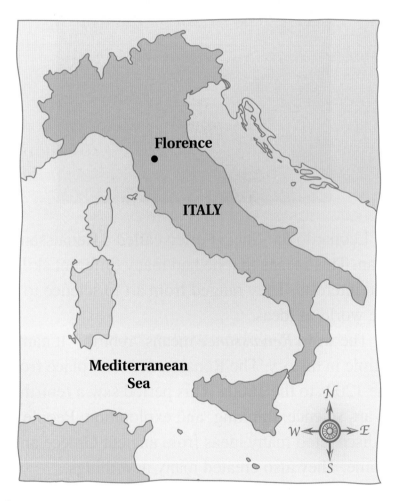

Florence

ITALY

Mediterranean Sea

Would you have gone to school?

If you had rich parents, you would have had an education. You might have had private lessons at home.

Leonardo did not have rich parents and, therefore, did not have much education. Still, he did learn to read and write. In his day, not everyone in Florence had books. The printing press had been invented in 1452, a few years before Leonardo was born. He came up with a better design. It was a press that one person could run.

If your family was not rich, you would probably have studied a trade (if you were a boy, that is). In the city of Florence, guilds were important. Guilds were like trade unions today. Young workers in a guild learned their skills at the feet of older, experienced workers. Each guild was specialized. You might have become a stonecutter or weaver, for example.

One important craft in Leonardo's city was painting. At this time, most artists worked in workshops where they were told what to paint. They did not get to plan their own pictures or sign their work. Many artists might have worked on one painting.

Renaissance painters tried to paint things the way they looked in real life. This was a big change from the art from the Middle Ages. Earlier art showed people and places, but the subjects looked flat. Real objects and people have height, width, and depth. Renaissance artists tried to show objects with lifelike proportions. They painted people making realistic gestures.

When Leonardo was fourteen or fifteen, he joined the workshop of a famous artist named Verrocchio. Some of Leonardo's first jobs were probably cleaning brushes and sweeping the floor. Later he ground colors to make paint. After a few years, he began to paint and sculpt.

Art of the Middle Ages looks flat.

Lady with an Ermine, a painting done by Leonardo in 1485

In this workshop, Leonardo also learned to work with metal to make statues. One time, Verrocchio was asked to build a statue of a large horse. The work was never completed. Leonardo would later plan his own bronze horse statue for the Duke of Milan.

Leonardo often mixed science with art. To paint the human body properly, he studied the bodies of dead people. He got in trouble for doing this, but he learned a lot about how human bodies worked.

Verrocchio

How would you have told time in Renaissance Florence?

If you lived in Leonardo's city, you could have heard bells ringing in the *campanile*. This was the tall bell tower that housed the church bells. There were clocks during the Renaissance, but few people owned them. The bells let people know when to go to work or to church. Different bells rang at different times of the day.

Leonardo was known as an inventor as well as a painter. He made a new kind of clock. His clock had a minute hand.

Leonardo loved animals, especially horses. This is one of his many sketches of horses.

What would you have eaten during the Renaissance?

During the Renaissance, no one had a refrigerator! Food spoiled easily without a way to keep it cool. Spices were used to cover the taste of spoiled foods. The need for nutmeg, ginger, pepper, and cloves led to the spice trade around the world. This trade led to the explorations of lands beyond Italy that proved that the world was round.

If you lived in Leonardo's city, you probably would have eaten pasta, as he did. You might have eaten it with oil and nuts instead of tomato sauce. People also ate meat, but not Leonardo. He loved animals so much that he became a vegetarian.

What kind of clothing would you have worn?

If you lived during the Renaissance, you would not have worn pants! Men often wore tight, colorful leggings and a long shirt. Women wore long gowns. Pearls and fur decorated the dresses of the wealthy women of Florence.

Leonardo's city was known for its colorful woolens and silks. Cloth from Florence was sold all over Europe. Many workers dyed the cloth bright colors. At the time of Leonardo's death, they began using dried beetles to make one colorful dye!

Someone once described Leonardo wearing a rose-colored outfit, but we don't know what he wore most of the time. We do know he made fun of some Renaissance styles.

Where would you have lived?

In Leonardo's time, some people lived in cities. Many lived in the country. Leonardo was born in the village of Vinci. That's where he got his name—Leonardo da Vinci.

Wealthy people in the city of Florence lived behind high walls. Courtyards or gardens formed the center of their property.

Verrocchio's workshop was Leonardo's home much of the time he was in Florence. He must have liked city living. After he left Florence, he spent many years traveling between that city and the city of Milan.

Florence was a city of 100,000 people in Leonardo's time.

How would you have gotten from place to place?

There were no cars or trains or planes in Leonardo's city. Most people walked from place to place. That was easy since few people who lived in Florence ever left the city. If you walked around Leonardo's city, you could have used an odometer that he designed. This tool would have measured the distance you traveled.

Leonardo could envision transportation of the future. His notebooks showed sketches for a bicycle, much like those we ride today. He sketched a car. He designed a flying machine. He even tried to fly! Leonardo's notebooks were secret. He was left-handed and wrote his notes backwards. As a result, no one else could read them.

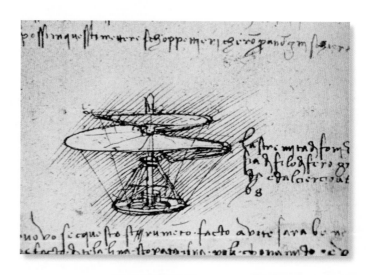

Cosimo and Lorenzo de Medici

Who was in charge of Renaissance Florence?

As Renaissance merchants became more successful, they also became more powerful. In Leonardo's city, the Medici family was the most powerful. Cosimo de Medici had envisioned a grand city. Florence was becoming that place. Cosimo hired painters and architects to design works of art.

Battles raged as some people resisted the power of the Medicis. These rebels could have used some of the machines that Leonardo designed. He drew a tank and a ladder for climbing tall walls.

Eventually, Lorenzo, Cosimo's grandson, came into power. He was interested in poetry and songs.

Leonardo da Vinci's *Mona Lisa,* one of the world's most famous paintings

Leaving the Renaissance City

In 1481, Leonardo decided it was time to leave Florence. He wanted to work for a new boss, the Duke of Milan. Although Leonardo would return to Florence many times in his heart, he had moved on. He would create his most famous works out-side of Florence, including the *Mona Lisa.* He also began his never-completed statue of a giant horse in Milan.

Leonardo was a skilled man who learned a lot from his time in the city of Florence. His life was and still is a symbol of the Renaissance.

Think Critically

1. Retell the important events in Leonardo da Vinci's life in order.

2. What is the author's main purpose in writing this book?

3. What about Leonardo made him a symbol of the Renaissance?

4. Why doesn't this book include any photographs of people?

5. What do you think of Leonardo's painting, *Mona Lisa?*

 Social Studies

Florence Today Do research on the Internet or use other library sources to compare life in Florence today to Leonardo's Florence. Make a chart that shows how Florence today is the same and how it is different from Leonardo's Florence.

School-Home Connection Tell family members three things about the Renaissance. Then talk about any statues or landmarks in your town. Plan to visit one together.

Word Count: 1,304 (with graphic 1,308)